INCREDIBLY DISGUSTING DRUGS

INHALANTS AND YOUR NASAL PASSAGES
The Incredibly Disgusting Story

Kerri O'Donnell

the rosen publishing group's
rosen central
new york

Published in 2001 by The Rosen Publishing Group, Inc.
29 East 21st Street, New York, NY 10010

First Edition

Library of Congress Cataloging-in-Publication Data

O'Donnell, Kerri, 1972–
Inhalants and your nasal passages: the incredibly disgusting story / by Kerri O'Donnell. — 1st ed.
p.; cm. — (Incredibly disgusting drugs)
Includes bibliographical references and index.
ISBN 0-8239-3392-X (library binding)
1. Solvent abuse—Juvenile literature. 2. Solvents—Health aspects—Juvenile literature. 3. Substance abuse—Prevention—Juvenile literature.
[1. Solvent abuse. 2. Substance abuse.]
[DNLM: 1. Administration, Inhalation—Adolescence—Popular Works.
2. Street Drugs—adverse effects—Popular Works. 3. Nasal Cavity—drug effects—Popular Works. 4. Solvents—adverse effects—Popular Works.
5. Substance-Related Disorders—Adolescence—Popular Works. WM 270 O263i 2001] I. Title. II. Series.
RC568.S64 O36 2001
362.29'9—dc21

00-011612

Manufactured in the United States of America

CONTENTS

Introduction 4

1 Everybody's Doing It 6

2 Inhalants—A Big Word for a Big Problem 11

3 Your Nasal Passages: The Gateway to Disaster 15

4 The Warning Signs 26

5 To Die For? 35

Glossary 42
For More Information 43
For Further Reading 46
Index 47

Introduction

Megan was thirteen years old the first time she got high on inhalants. She was at her friend Serena's house, watching movies and painting her nails. Soon, they were sniffing the nail polish remover and giggling. It made them feel light-headed and silly. They didn't think that they were doing anything harmful; after all, you could buy nail polish remover at the store for less than two dollars. It wasn't illegal, and it wasn't a "drug."

The next day at school, they told a friend about what they'd done and how fun it was.

"You should try breathing cooking spray out of a paper bag," their friend Brian said. "Tim and I laughed so hard. Glue works good, too. And correction fluid is a blast."

Megan and Serena started to experiment. They sniffed glue, correction fluid, and felt-tip

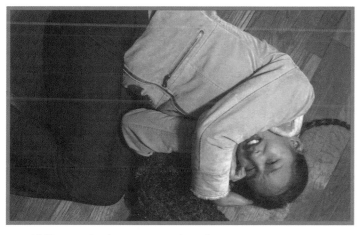
Sniffing inhalants can lead to very serious health problems.

markers. They tried paint thinner, but that made them feel a bit sick. They breathed cooking spray out of paper bags. They sucked in the air from whipped cream canisters. They told their friends about it, and soon they all started meeting at Serena's house to "huff" different things out of paper bags. They'd laugh for what seemed like hours. And best of all, they didn't think they were doing anything bad.

One day, Serena and Megan sniffed some hair spray in Serena's room. Serena felt woozy, so she sat back and waited for the feeling to pass. That's when she noticed that Megan was lying on the floor, shaking. Serena ran to get her parents. Her parents were worried that maybe Megan was having a seizure. They rushed Megan to the hospital, where she ended up staying for several days.

Megan was going to be okay, the doctors said, but she was lucky. She could have died.

1 Everybody's Doing It

"Cooking spray? Glue? Paint thinner? That's totally gross," you might say. "Who'd want to inhale any of that stuff?"

Most people agree. But the sad truth is, a lot of people—many of whom are your age or even younger—are doing it every day, and they're damaging their bodies and minds in the process. Some are even dying because of inhalants.

I JUST WANT TO FIT IN

Chances are you know someone who uses inhalants on a regular basis. You may have even tried using inhalants yourself. You're at an age when a lot of people are going to be telling you that you're not "cool" unless you do certain things like smoking cigarettes, drinking alcohol, or doing drugs. Not only are you probably trying to figure out how to feel comfortable in your own skin, but you're probably trying to find your place in the world, too. You might suddenly be worried about what everyone else thinks of you.

With all of this going on, when a friend or classmate tells you that you should sniff glue or spray paint because "everybody's doing it" and it'll make you feel good, it's understandable that you might be tempted to go ahead and try it. "Why not?" you may think. Maybe you're afraid people might think you're a loser if you refuse. The truth of the matter is that the way to be cool is to keep yourself healthy and strong. You've got a lot to look forward to in life. However, continue that huffing and you'll be irreparably damaging your nasal passages, your brain, your liver, your kidneys, and even your central nervous system. In other words, you may not have a long healthy life to enjoy, no matter how cool you or anyone else may think you are.

THE SAD TRUTH

The statistics are astounding. Inhalants are among the substances most commonly abused by young people today. In the National Household Survey on Drug Abuse conducted in

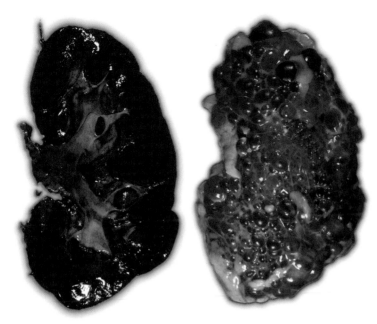

A healthy kidney *(left)* and a damaged kidney *(right)*.

1996, 1.3 million adolescents (6 percent) said they had used inhalants at least once in their lives, and 900,000 (4 per-cent) adoles-cents said that they had used some type of inhalant in the past year. The National Institute of Drug Abuse (NIDA) estimates that one in five people will use inhalants by the time he or she reaches the eighth grade. There have even been reports of children as young as five or six years old using inhalants.

RIGHT UNDER YOUR NOSE

Why is the use of inhalants so widespread? For one thing, young people often use inhalants as a substitute for liquor, since inhalants are easier to get and cheaper to buy. A very young child can stumble across an inhalant without even

Inhalants are especially dangerous because they are found in many household cleaning products.

realizing that he or she is doing anything dangerous. You don't have to find a drug dealer to get your inhalant of choice because inhalants aren't really drugs. Inhalants are toxins, or poisons—and they're all around you.

They're Everywhere—Even in Your House

You may not have realized this before, but inhalants can be found under your kitchen sink in the form of household cleaning products and air fresheners. They're in your kitchen cabinets in the form of cooking spray. They can be found in your refrigerator in the form of whipped-cream canisters or in your bathroom in the form of hair spray. They're on your

> Inhalants are the fourth most abused substance among young people ages seven to seventeen. Only alcohol, tobacco, and marijuana abuse are more prevalent. Because inhalant abusers tend to start at a young age, inhalants can serve as a stepping stone to more substance abuse in later years.

garage shelf in the form of spray paint and paint thinner. They're even in your desk at school in the form of correction fluid and markers. The list goes on and on.

Experts have estimated that there are more than 1,000 substances that can be used as inhalants. These substances are, for the most part, entirely legal to buy. They're generally pretty cheap, too. When used for the purposes for which they were initially manufactured, many of these substances are useful to us. When they're misused, they can hurt us.

Because these products are so easily available, it's hard to monitor how they are used. It's even more difficult to monitor how they're misused. You need to know what inhalants are and all of the truly awful things that they can do to you. Then you will be better equipped to decide what you think is cool to do.

2 Inhalants—A Big Word for a Big Problem

An inhalant is a chemical that produces fumes that can be inhaled, or breathed in. When these fumes are breathed in, they produce mind-altering effects. The person inhaling the fumes may feel giddy and lightheaded at first, and might like the way this feels. The person might feel kind of drunk or "high" from the fumes. With this feeling may come a sense of happiness. The user might feel more outgoing and uninhibited, or like he or she is on top of the world—at least for a little while. What people often don't realize is that inhalants are damaging to their insides.

Like Serena and Megan, most people who abuse inhalants don't think that there's anything wrong with what they're doing. "I just sniffed some spray paint," a user might say. "What's the big deal? It's not like it's cocaine or anything."

Wrong. You can get hooked on inhalants just as easily as you can get hooked on cocaine or any other drug. Inhalants can damage everything from your nasal passages to your brain, liver, kidneys, and central nervous system. They can also damage your bone marrow—the tissue in your bones that produces new blood cells. And, like we said before, inhalants can kill you.

Not convinced? You will be.

THE DIFFERENT TYPES OF INHALANTS

Inhalants fall into four main categories—solvents (often called volatile solvents), aerosols, anesthetics, and nitrites.

 A volatile solvent is a substance—such as nail polish remover, gasoline, paint thinner, cleaning fluid, lighter fluid, or correction fluid—in which other things dissolve. Solvents affect the body much like depressants do—by slowing down the activity of the central nervous system.

Healthy bone marrow *(left)* and damaged, cancerous bone marrow *(right)* resulting from sniffing paint thinner *(center)*.

 An aerosol is a combination of a liquid and a propellant, which pushes the liquid out of an aerosol can. Hair spray, spray paint, some kinds of perfume, air fresheners, and cooking spray are aerosols. Propellants in aerosols are made of fluorocarbons, which also act like depressants.

 An anesthetic is a substance that is used to dull pain. It can come in the form of liquid or gas. Ether, chloroform, and nitrous oxide are some examples of anesthetics. Ether and chloroform are sometimes found in lighter fluids and cleaning fluids. Nitrous oxide is an anesthetic gas that is also commonly used as a propellant in cans of whipped cream.

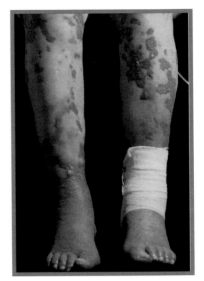

Inhalant abuse can cause Kaposi's Sarcoma.

 Nitrites are chemicals that dilate the heart's blood vessels. Amyl nitrite (a kind of nitrite) was once commonly used to treat heart problems. The small vials of amyl nitrite also produce a quick euphoric feeling when inhaled. Nitrites are often called "poppers" or "snappers" because of what they sound like when they are broken open and inhaled. Some room fresheners contain a type of nitrite called butyl nitrite. Amyl and butyl nitrites have been linked with a cancer called Kaposi's sarcoma.

Now you've got the information you need about all the different types of inhalants. What happens when you actually inhale any of these things? You're about to find out.

3 Your Nasal Passages: The Gateway to Disaster

Even though inhalants are grouped into different classes, almost all of them affect the body like anesthetics—they slow down the body's functions. Outwardly, inhalants can (and usually do) make you feel intoxicated, and this feeling can last for a few minutes or many hours, depending on how often the inhalants are used. Inhalants can give you a headache, make you dizzy and lightheaded, or can make you feel very sleepy, disoriented, or confused. They can make you stumble around when you walk and can make you slur your speech. Hmm, inhalants kind of seem less cool than you thought, right?

Accidents can occur after sniffing inhalants.

HOW INHALANTS WORK—AN OVERVIEW

Even though those awful reactions are bad enough—imagine feeling so light-headed that you fall off your bike and get hit by a car—what inhalants do to your insides, starting with your nasal passages, is even worse.

Let's go through this step by step so you can see just what we mean. One of the most common ways to abuse inhalants is to sniff them through the nose.

YOUR NOSE

First, take a moment to consider your nose. You probably don't ever think a whole lot about your nose. It just sits there on your face, and the only time you notice it is when you've got a cold and it's stuffed up, or if it has a big zit on it and you're so mortified that you don't ever want to leave your room again. However, your nose is a pretty complex structure. Breathe in through your nose. Now breathe out. Do it again. Right now, your nose is being used as it should be— to breathe in air and get oxygen to your lungs and the rest of your body. This process is called respiration.

During respiration, your lungs take in oxygen, then pass the oxygen into your blood. Your blood then delivers the oxygen to your organs and tissues. Your body needs oxygen to live. Deprive yourself of oxygen for even a few minutes and you die. You go brain dead. Your heart stops. It's all over. It's that simple. And it can happen the very first time you try an inhalant.

NASAL PASSAGES

Let's explore the inside of your nose, since this is the gateway to the process of respiration. If you were to take a trip up your own nostrils (not that you'd want to), you'd see what are called nasal passages. The nasal passages lead to an open area called the nasal cavity. This is where the air you breathe in is warmed before it moves down your throat to your lungs.

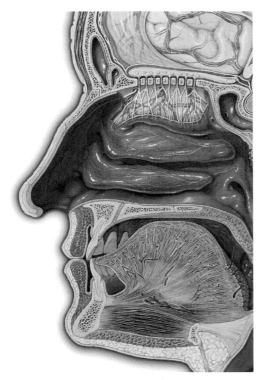

Mucous membranes in our nasal passages alert our brains when germs enter our bodies.

This entire passageway between your nostrils and your lungs is lined with a mucous membrane. The mucous membrane has many functions. It helps you sense odors so you can smell things. It can also spot viruses and germs that have come into your body. White blood cells can then attack these viruses and germs to help keep you from getting sick.

I Smell Trouble

When you sniff inhalants, you risk damaging your nose, your throat, your lungs, and every organ in your body that blood is carried to, including your heart and brain.

Imagine a container of paint thinner. You know what the stuff smells like from a distance . . . how can you miss it if your mom or dad is doing some painting

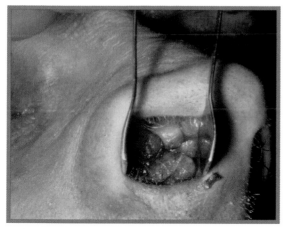
When used for a long time, inhalants can cause damage to a user's nose.

around the house? Pretty gross, right? Not something you'd want anywhere near your nose, let alone your insides. And let's not forget that it can eat right through paint, too.

Think of what it would be like to permanently damage or lose your sense of smell. Just imagine what inhaling vapors from paint thinner close up can do to your nose, since that's the first passage the pain thinner has got to go through before it makes its way to the rest of your body. Imagine the paint thinner eating through the mucous membrane that lines your nose and throat. Picture your nose running all over the place, uncontrollably and all of the time. Think of having a painful, inflamed nose more often than not. Visualize getting terrible nosebleeds when you least expect them. And there's more. Imagine getting gross, oozing, rashlike sores inside and around your nose and above your upper lip. Still like inhalants?

WHAT HAPPENS NEXT?

Once you've sniffed an inhalant, the damage it does to your nose is just the beginning. As the vapors from the inhalant move down to your lungs, they can damage the soft tissues of your throat, too. Inhalants containing fluoro-carbons (aerosols and propellants) can even freeze the inside of your throat, which can make it hard to breathe. This can lead to death.

Inhalants deprive your lungs of needed oxygen. They can coat the surface of the lungs and make it impossible for your lungs to absorb oxygen. If your lungs have no oxygen, they can't deliver oxygen to the heart, brain, and other organs via your blood. The possible result? Suffocation.

Brain Pain

Your brain controls your body functions—including every-thing from how your heart beats and how you blink your eyes, to how you cry at a sad movie or how you solve a really tough math problem. If you damage your brain, you damage the quality of your life and give up some (if not most) of the things your body is currently able to do on its own. When you use some kinds of inhalants, the chemicals they contain attack your brain, causing nerve damage.

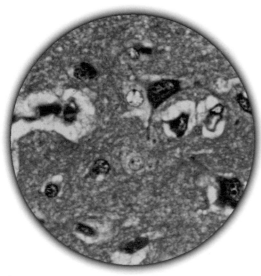

Long-term use of inhalants damaged these neurons.

Your brain is covered with a fatty tissue called myelin. Myelin protects many of the body's nerve cells—or neurons—that are located in the brain. Neurons send and receive messages and control almost everything that your body does, including every-thing that you think. Many inhalants—like cleaning sol-vents—are actually products that are meant to break down and remove fats and oils. When the chemicals in these inhalants reach the brain, they attack the fatty myelin layer of the brain in the same way. Chronic use of inhalants can break down myelin and can make it impossible for neurons to give and receive messages to the rest of the body.

Ready to Go Out of Your Mind?

If this happens in the cerebral cortex, the outermost part of the cerebrum (which makes up about 85 percent of the brain), your problem-solving abilities may be impaired and your personality may drastically change—permanently. If

Inhalants can affect your brain and your body in adverse ways.

this happens in the cerebellum, located at the back of the cerebrum, you may lose coordination and bodily control, causing you to become clumsy and slow. You may experience tremors and uncontrollable shaking. Your memory may also be affected. A chronic inhalant abuser may not be able to recognize things that should be familiar, may be unable to learn new things, and may no longer be able to participate in even the simplest conversation. Doesn't sound like so much fun, does it?

The Heart of the Matter

Many inhalants dilate the blood vessels so that more blood can flow through them. Some inhalants can also increase your heart rate, and some make the heart very sensitive to the hormone epinephrine. If a person has a sudden scare

After you use an inhalant, it takes a while before your body is able to get rid of what you've taken into your system. On average, it takes about twelve hours for your body to eliminate just half of what you sniff. The remaining toxins can remain in your system for more than two days, affecting all of your organs—your lungs, kidneys, and liver, to name just a few.

or is surprised while using inhalants, the body may release epinephrine. This can cause a wildly erratic heartbeat and may even lead to death from cardiac arrest. This is called sudden sniffing death syndrome. It's a technical term that means you're just plain dead.

Equal Opportunity Poisons

It started with just sniffing something up your nose, and look where it has gotten you. By this point, you probably get the picture. We'll wrap up all the doom and gloom with other disgusting facts about what inhalants can do to your body.

- Some inhalants can affect the ophthalmic nerve, impairing sight.

- Chronic abusers may experience reduced muscle mass, tone, and strength.

- Benzene, a chemical found in gasoline, affects the bone marrow. Some benzene abusers develop leukemia, a cancer of the bone marrow.

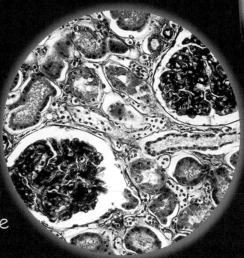

Leukemia in a kidney cell

- Repeated use of nitrous oxide (whipped cream propellant) and hexane (a component in some fuels and glues) can impair the peripheral nervous system. Users may experience a tingling sensation, numbness, or complete paralysis.

- Chronic abusers may experience severe mood swings and may act violently.

- Some inhalants can damage the acoustic nerve, which may cause deafness.

- Inhalant use over a long period may cause the abuser to lose control of his or her bowels.

- Long-term abuse can cause irreparable kidney and liver damage.

- Some inhalants can make the user feel afraid, guilty, and even lonely.

- Long-term abuse of inhalants can cause uncontrollable hand tremors, drooling, and bad breath.

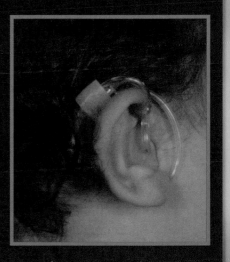

Your hearing can be affected by using inhalants.

4 The Warning Signs

One of the most frightening things about inhalants is that it can be very hard to tell that someone has a problem. Because products that can be used as inhalants are so common, most people don't take much notice of the fact that these items may be turning up in strange places—a can of spray paint next to the bed, for instance, or model airplane glue in the backpack of someone who doesn't even own a model airplane.

However, there are definite signs to look out for that can clue you in to whether someone you know is putting his or her life on the line for a cheap "high."

Inhalant users often keep products like spray paint and glue in places that others may consider odd.

NOT JUST SNIFFING AROUND

Before we get into what you should be on the lookout for, let's discuss two alternatives to sniffing. Then you'll have a better grasp of what to be on the lookout for.

Bagging It

People who use inhalants often use a method called bagging. This term is pretty self-explanatory. It basically means that a substance (like glue, for instance) is put inside a paper or plastic bag, or a balloon. Then the bag or balloon

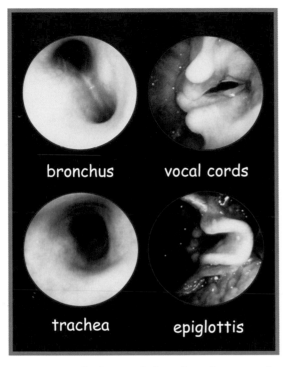

bronchus   vocal cords

trachea   epiglottis

Images of the epiglottis, the vocal cords, and the interiors of the trachea and the bronchus.

is fitted around the nose and mouth, and the fumes are inhaled. When inhalants containing fluorocarbons are placed inside a bag, they can turn to liquid, in part. If this happens, the likelihood of damaging the tissue in your throat greatly increases, and breathing can become extremely difficult. Because the toxic fumes become so concentrated when the bagging method is used, the frequency of death is even greater.

Huffing and Puffing

Another method of inhaling is called huffing. A huffer takes a sock, a wad of toilet paper, or a rag, and soaks it in whatever substance is to be inhaled. The sock, toilet paper, or rag is then stuck inside the mouth and the huffer inhales through his or her mouth. Sounds appetizing, doesn't it? Imagine having a mouth full of cleaning solution. The vapors from the chemical being inhaled are awful enough, but accidental ingestion of the chemical itself is extremely dangerous, too.

HOW TO SPOT A USER

We're going to give you the benefit of the doubt and assume that you care too much about yourself to use inhalants. But since the problem is so widespread, you may know someone who is abusing inhalants. Sometimes the signs are obvious, but sometimes they are much more subtle.

A Helping Hand for Harris

Rajiv and Harris had sat next to each other in homeroom for two years. They didn't have the same friends, but they often ate lunch together, and they always talked on the phone after school. Rajiv liked Harris because he was a nice, outgoing guy who always had a joke or funny story to tell.

The change in Harris happened so gradually that Rajiv didn't really notice it at first. In the mornings during homeroom, Harris didn't seem his usual self. He looked sort of spaced out, his eyes gazing off into the distance at nothing in particular. Then Harris stopped eating lunch with Rajiv, and he didn't call him anymore, either. In fact, Harris didn't seem to talk to anyone anymore.

Rajiv thought that maybe Harris was in a bad mood about something. Harris had broken up with his girlfriend a few months earlier, and maybe he was still sad about that. Or maybe there was something going on with his family. Rajiv didn't want to ask. He figured that it was none of his business and that Harris would tell him if he wanted to.

One day, Rajiv saw Harris coming out of the bathroom looking all red-eyed. Harris walked right by him and stumbled a bit as he continued down the hall. Maybe he wasn't feeling well, Rajiv thought.

Weeks later, during homeroom, Rajiv took a long, hard look at Harris. There were reddish sores under his nose and above his lip. It looked like he had a rash. In fact, the skin in that area looked kind of discolored. Something weird was going on. Rajiv had heard of a few kids sniffing spray paint and glue in the bathrooms at school, but he had never seen it happen. Maybe Harris had gotten himself into some trouble with that stuff. Rajiv decided that he'd casually talk to Harris's mom (who worked at the school library) to see if she had sensed anything weird.

When he talked to Mrs. Malloy, he decided that he had better tell her about his suspicions. He was pretty sure that Harris was huffing, and he'd even tried to talk to him himself, but Harris had blown him off. Telling Mrs. Malloy what *was up was the only way he could think of to make sure that his friend got some help.*

WHAT TO LOOK FOR

Rajiv could also have talked to a teacher or a guidance counselor. The point is, he told someone who could make sure that Harris got the help he needed. It's important to be aware of the warning signs of inhalant abuse so that you can help someone before it's too late.

Warning Signs

People who abuse inhalants may think that no one could possibly know what they're doing behind closed doors, but the signs eventually make an appearance. Here are just a few:

- Increased tendency toward anxious, irritable, or easily excitable behavior
- Depression
- Excessive fatigue
- Memory lapses and/or confusion
- Lack of concentration
- Violent outbursts and/or severe mood swings

Abusing inhalants can make the user appear to be dazed or intoxicated.

- A drunken appearance
- Lack of concern about appearance
- Frequent complaints of headaches
- Noticeable weight loss and decrease in appetite
- Abdominal pain or frequent feelings of nausea
- Vomiting and/or diarrhea
- A chemical odor coming from the individual
- Eyes that are red or watery
- A red or runny nose or frequent nosebleeds
- Excessive sneezing and/or coughing

- Tremors in the hands
- Reddish, rashlike sores around the nostrils and mouth
- Paint stains on the individual's body or clothes or discoloration of the skin

If you notice that someone is exhibiting even a few of these symptoms, get help fast. You might be wrong, but that's actually the best news there could be! If you're right, you'll be saving someone's life.

When It's in Your Hands

What if you're present when a person is sniffing, bagging, or huffing? There are a few things you should know if you find yourself in this situation. The main thing is to keep yourself and the user calm. Panicking can cause the user to become violent. It is best to avoid causing any kind of excitement or stress at all—this can cause an irregular heartbeat in the inhaler, which could lead to sudden sniffing death (cardiac arrest).

If the person is conscious, the most important thing is to make sure the room is well ventilated so that any harmful fumes can't do further damage. If the person is unconscious or appears to have stopped breathing, immediately

In some cases of inhalant abuse, paramedics might need to be called.

call for help and perform CPR—cardiopulmonary resuscitation, a first-aid procedure that maintains a person's breathing and blood circulation—until help comes. Try to find out what type of inhalant was used by looking around the room or talking to witnesses. Paramedics will need to know this information so they can treat the person appropriately.

When the person (hopefully) recovers, it's time to get him or her the professional help needed to deal with the addiction. Try to get the person to speak to a health care professional—whether it's a doctor, psychologist, school counselor or nurse, or substance abuse counselor—so that he or she can start dealing with the problem.

5 To Die For?

By now it should be clear that inhalants can damage your body and mind beyond repair. The lure of fitting in and being cool just isn't worth it. You already know about the physical changes that take place in your body, but there's another aspect of inhalant abuse to consider—addiction.

LONG-TERM EFFECTS

After continued abuse of inhalants, you can no longer get the same effect by inhaling the same amount. You've got to take it to the next level and inhale even more poisonous fumes just to get the same results. This is because a chronic user develops what is called a tolerance.

If you decided you were going to run five miles each day, starting tomorrow, you might feel out of breath after the first mile and have to force yourself to keep going. Eventually, though, you would be running five miles without having to put so much effort into it. Your body would get used to the activity, and you would have to increase your mileage to get the same kind of physical workout.

When you use inhalants, your body adapts in much the same way, but obviously the results are not beneficial like the effects of exercise. Quite simply, the more you use, the more you'll need a bigger hit of poison.

Inhaling from a bag can cause asphyxiation.

The Last Hurrah

Experts estimate that inhalants play a part in more than 100 deaths each year just in the United States alone. These deaths usually occur when people inhale very strong concentrations of fumes. If you've developed a tolerance from chronic abuse of inhalants, you'll have to keep upping the amount you inhale, strengthening the concentration of fumes. You're more likely to die as a result. That's not to say that inhaling "just a little" isn't as dangerous—using inhalants just once can kill you.

How Death Comes Knocking

Most medical experts agree that inhalants can cause death in several different ways.

The user can die of asphyxiation. When fumes limit the amount of oxygen in the air, breathing can stop altogether. The user then suffocates. This usually happens in situations where the user inhales from a bag. The high concentration of fumes in the bag can stop respiration.

The user can die by choking on his or her own vomit as a result of inhaling poisonous fumes.

The user can die of sudden sniffing death syndrome. The heart is thrown into an irregular rhythm and cardiac arrest can occur. Some experts say that there is a greater risk of sudden death with a single dose of inhalants than there is with any other drug.

The user can die when the use of inhalants clouds his or her judgment and/or ability to function properly.

Using inhalants can cloud one's judgment and lead to fatal results, especially while driving.

For example, a person under the influence of inhalants might lose consciousness while driving a car and have a fatal accident. That person could also kill an innocent bystander.

KICKING THE HABIT

Obviously, the best thing that a chronic abuser can do is to stop using inhalants before it's too late. However, it's important to know that you can't just walk away from months or years of regular inhalant abuse without your body responding in some way—usually a negative way—to this new development.

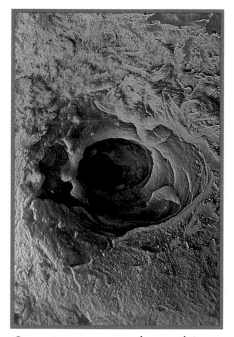

Sweat pores, such as this one, may overreact during inhalant withdrawal.

When a person who has been abusing inhalants stops using them, the body reacts by going through a process called withdrawal. Because the body has by this point built up a tolerance, it begins to expect the physical effects that the inhalants' poisons bring. It is a physical dependence, but it is also a psychological dependence—the user craves those familiar feelings. When the inhalants don't come, the body reacts, and it's not a pretty picture.

People experiencing inhalant withdrawal are likely to experience tremors in their hands. They may become very nervous and agitated. They may sweat profusely or have the chills. They may experience severe chronic headaches and muscle cramps, or have difficulty sleeping. Some people experience hallucinations. On top of all of this, they may feel nauseous and experience problems with their bowels. The point is: If you never start using inhalants to begin with, you won't have to stop, so your body will never be put through the withdrawal wringer.

A Rough Road Ahead

Abusing inhalants is a tough habit to break. Statistics show that young people who have a history of chronic abuse are often unsuccessful in getting the proper treatment for the problem. When compared to abusers of other drugs, inhalant abusers have a much higher percentage of treatment failure and subsequent relapse. Inhalant abusers need to be treated for longer periods of time to achieve any kind of success. This is because most users need between thirty and forty days to get the toxins out of their systems. This is called detoxification.

BE BRAVE, BE STRONG . . . BE HEALTHY

Perhaps the most important piece of advice we can give you is really the simplest advice: Be good to yourself and treat yourself with respect. Have confidence in your abilities and use them, rather than abusing inhalants or any other substance in order to be accepted by other people. Those other people aren't nearly as cool as they would have you believe. They're poisoning their bodies and minds, perhaps even permanently.

If you feel that you need to use inhalants or any other drug, including alcohol, to feel confident about yourself, it means that there is a bigger problem that needs to be addressed—your self-esteem. Drugs can't solve your problems, they can only make you forget about them for a little while. Drugs can't change you into the person you wish you were—they can only trick you into believing that they can.

When all is said and done, abusing drugs makes your problems so much worse. If you feel you need to escape from your problems for a little while, go see a movie or sit under a tree and read a good book. Go for a hike and think about the wonderful life that's out there for you if you want it. Talk to someone about your feelings. Remember that you're in charge. Make sure you stay that way!

GLOSSARY

anesthetic Substance that causes numbness in all or part of the body.

asphyxiation Unconsciousness or death caused by lack of oxygen or excess of carbon dioxide—usually caused by interruption of breathing.

bagging Inhaling substances from a plastic or paper bag to get high.

central nervous system Part of the nervous system made up of the brain and spinal cord.

cerebellum Part of the brain that controls the body's balance and the coordination of muscles.

depressant Drug that slows down the nervous system's normal activity.

epinephrine Hormone secreted by the adrenal glands that acts as a heart stimulant.

ether Liquid used as a solvent and an anesthetic.

fluorocarbon Compound used in lubricants, refrigerants, and cooking spray.

Kaposi's sarcoma Disease affecting the skin and mucous membranes.

myelin Soft, white, fatty material covering the nerve fibers in the brain.

neuron Nerve cell.

nitrous oxide Colorless gas that produces a loss of sensibility to pain when inhaled, preceded by a feeling of giddiness. Nitrous oxide is sometimes used as an anesthetic in dentistry.

propellant Pressurized gas.

FOR MORE INFORMATION

In the United States

American Council for Drug
   Education
164 West 74th Street
New York, NY 10023
(800) DRUG-HELP (378-4435)
Web site: http://www.acde.org
e-mail: acde@phoenix-
   house.org

Center for Substance Abuse
   Prevention (CSAP)
1010 Wayne Avenue, Suite 850
Silver Spring, MD 20910
(301) 459-1591, ext. 244
Web site: http://covesoft.com/
   csap.html

Community Anti-Drug
   Coalitions of America
901 North Pitt Street, Suite 300
Alexandria, VA 22314
(800) 54-CADCA (542-2322)
Web site: http://www.cadca.org

National Center on Addiction
   and Substance Abuse at
   Columbia University.
633 Third Avenue, 19th Floor
New York, NY 10017-6706
(212) 841-5200
Web site: http://www.
   casacolumbia.org

National Clearinghouse for
   Alcohol and Drug
   Information
PO Box 2345
Rockville, MD 20847-2345
(800) SAY-NOTO (729-6686)
Web site:
   http://www.health.org

National Council on
   Alcoholism and Drug
   Dependence, Inc.
12 West 21st Street
New York, NY 10010
(212) 206-6770
(800) NCA-CALL (622-2255)
Web site:
   http://www.ncadd.org
e-mail: national@ncadd.org

National Inhalant Prevention
   Coalition
1201 West Sixth Street,
   Room C-200
Austin, TX 78703
(800) 269-4237
Web site:
   http://www.inhalants.org
e-mail: nipc@io.com

National Institute on Drug
   Abuse (NIDA)

6001 Executive Boulevard
Bethesda, MD 20892
Room 5213
(301) 443-1124
Web site:
   http://www.nida.nih.gov

PRIDE Youth Programs
4684 South Evergreen
Newaygo, MI 49337
(231) 652-4400
Web site:
   http://www.prideusa.org
e-mail:
   prideyouth@ncats.net

Substance Abuse and
   Mental Health Services
   Administration
Room 12-105, Parklawn
   Building
5600 Fishers Lane
Rockville, MD 20857

Web site:
  http://www.samhsa.gov

Youth Power (formerly, Just
  Say No)
2000 Franklin Street, Suite 400
Oakland, CA 94612-2908
(800) 258-2766
Web site: http://www.
  youthpower.org
e-mail:
  youth@youthpower.org

In Canada

Canadian Centre on
  Substance Abuse
75 Albert Street, Suite 300
Ottawa, ON K1P 5E7
(613) 235-4048
Web site: http://www.ccsa.ca

Recovery Counselling Services
4576 Yonge Street, Suite 425
Toronto, ON M2N 6N4
(416) 658-3288
Web site: http://www.
  recoverycounselling.on.ca
e-mail: sober@
  recoverycounselling.on.ca

Smart Kids Don't Do Drugs
  Society of Canada
(800) 883-7761
Web site:
  http://www.skddd.com
e-mail: info@skddd.com

FOR FURTHER READING

Glowa, John R. *Inhalants: The Toxic Fumes*. New York: Chelsea House Publishers, 1986.

Hurwitz, Sue, and Nancy Shnideman. *Drugs and Your Friends.* New York: The Rosen Publishing Group, Inc., 1995.

Monroe, Judy. *Inhalant Drug Dangers*. Springfield, NJ: Enslow Publishers, Inc., 1999.

Myers, Arthur. *Drugs and Emotions*. New York: The Rosen Publishing Group, Inc., 1996.

Rawls, Bea O'Donnell, and Gwen Johnson. *Drugs and Where to Turn*. New York: The Rosen Publishing Group, Inc., 1993.

Sherry, Clifford J. *Inhalants*. New York: The Rosen Publishing Group, Inc., 2001.

Weatherly, Myra. *Inhalants*. Springfield, NJ: Enslow Publishers, Inc., 1996.

INDEX

A

aerosol, 12, 13, 20
amyl nitrite, 14
anesthetics, 12, 13–14, 15
asphyxiation, 37

B

bagging, 27–28, 33
bone marrow, damage to, 12, 24
brain, damage to, 7, 12, 18, 20–22
butyl nitrite, 14

C

cardiac arrest, 23, 33, 37
central nervous system, damage to, 7, 12

D

death, 5, 6, 12, 17, 20, 23, 36, 37–38
detoxification, 40

F

fluorocarbons, 13, 20, 28

H

heart, damage to, 18, 20
heart rate/heartbeat, 22, 23, 33, 37
huffing, 5, 7, 28–29, 30, 33

K

kidneys, damage to, 7, 12, 25

L

liver, damage to, 7, 12, 25
lungs, damage to, 18, 20

M

mucous membrane, 18, 19
myelin, 21

N

nasal cavity, 17
nasal passages, 7, 12, 16, 17–18
National Household Survey on Drug Abuse, 7–8
National Institute of Drug Abuse, 8
neurons, 21
nitrites, 12, 14
nose, damage to, 18, 19, 20

P

"poppers"/"snappers," 14
propellants, 13, 14, 20

S

sudden death syndrome, 23, 33, 37
suffocation, 20, 37

T

throat, damage to, 18, 19, 20, 28
tolerance, 35–37, 39

V

volatile solvent, 12

W

warning signs of abuse, 31–33
withdrawal, 39

CREDITS

About the Author

Kerri O'Donnell received her degree in journalism from New York University. She is a writer and editor currently living in Buffalo, New York.

Photo Credits

Cover and 21 © R. Roseman/Custom Medical Stock Photo Inc., cover inset Antonio Mari; pp. 5, 9, 13 inset, 16, 22, 32, 36 Antonio Mari; p. 8 right © Peter Arnold, Inc.; p. 8 left © OJ Staats/Custom Medical Stock Photo, Inc.; p. 13 right © National Medical Slide Bank/Custom Medical Stock Photo; Inc. p. 13 left © Patricia Barber, RBP/Custom Medical Stock Photo; Inc. p. 14 © Zeva Oelbaum/Peter Arnold, Inc.; p. 18 © Professor Peter Cull/Science Photo Library; p. 19 © Biophoto Associates/Photo Researchers, Inc.; p.24 © Astrid & Hans-frieder Michler/Science Library; p. 25 © Custom Medical Stock Photo; Inc. p. 27 Cindy Reiman; p. 28 © Joseph R. Siebert, Ph.D./Custom Medical Stock Photo; Inc. p. 34 © Shout Pictures/Custom Medical Stock Photo; Inc. p.38 © L. O'Shaughnessy/H. Armstrong Roberts; p.39 © Dr. Jeremy Burgess/Science Photo Library.

Series Design

Laura Murawski